Jokes and Riddles

Where did Humpty Dumpty leave his hat?

Humpty dumped his hat on the wall.

What pet makes the loudest noise?

A trumpet.

Kingfisher Books, Grisewood & Dempsey Ltd,
Elsley House, 24–30 Great Titchfield Street, London W1P 7AD

First published in 1992 by Kingfisher Books.
2 4 6 8 10 9 7 5 3 1

Material in this edition was previously published by Kingfisher Books in *Animal Fun: Jokes and Riddles*, *Mik Brown's Joke Book*, *Mik Brown's Riddle Book* and *Mik Brown's Silly Riddles*

Copyright © Mik Brown 1983, 1986, 1987, 1992

All rights reserved.

BRITISH LIBRARY CATALOGUING-IN-PUBLICATION DATA
A catalogue record for this book is available from the British Library

ISBN 0 86272 972 6

Phototypeset by Waveney Typesetters, Norwich
Printed in Hong Kong by
South China Printing Company (1988) Limited

Jokes and Riddles

Mik Brown

"Doctor, doctor, I keep thinking I'm invisible."

"Who said that?"

Kingfisher Books

Why were the elephants thrown out of the swimming pool?

Why does an elephant wear sneakers?

So that he can sneak up on mice.

They couldn't hold their trunks up.

What do you call an elephant that flies?

Why are elephants so wrinkled?

Have you ever tried ironing one?

A Jumbo Jet.

What did the baby hedgehog say to the cactus?

"Is that you, Mum?"

Why did the hedgehog wear red boots?

Because his brown ones were at the menders.

BOING! BOING!

What's scaly, has a hard shell and bounces?

A tortoise on a pogo stick.

What was the tortoise doing on the motorway?

About 150 millimetres an hour.

"Waiter, waiter, is soup on the menu?"

"Waiter, waiter, bring me something to eat and make it snappy."

"How about a crocodile sandwich, sir?"

"No, madam, I wiped it off."

"Waiter, waiter, this egg is bad!"

"Don't blame me, madam, I only laid the table."

"Waiter, waiter, there's a fly in my soup!"

"Don't worry, sir, that spider on your bread will soon get rid of it."

What do you call a crate of ducks?

What do you call a gorilla wearing earphones?

Anything, he can't hear you.

YELL!

A box of quackers.

Why did the owl 'owl?

How did the monkey make toast?

He put it under the gorilla.

Because the woodpecker would peck 'er.

How does a sparrow with engine trouble manage to land safely?

With its sparrowchute.

What's black and white and red all over?

A sunburnt penguin.

What did the astronaut see in his frying pan?

An unidentified frying object.

SPLOP!

What do polar bears have for lunch?

Ice burgers.

What did the banana say to the monkey?

How do you catch a monkey?

Hang upside down in a tree and make a noise like a banana.

Nothing, bananas can't talk.

What's a crocodiles favourite card game?

Snap.

The dentist put his fingers in the crocodile's mouth to see how many teeth it had. What did the crocodile do?

It closed its mouth to see how many fingers the dentist had.

What do sea monsters eat?

Fish and ships.

What's big, red and prickly, has three eyes and eats rocks?

A big, red, prickly, three-eyed rock-eater.

What do you say when you meet a two-headed monster?

"Hello, Hello."

What has a purple-spotted body, hairy legs and big eyes on stalks?

I don't know, but there's one crawling up your leg.

What do you get
if you cross
a snake
with a magician?

Abra da cobra.

What do you get
if you cross a snowman
with a tiger?

Frostbite.

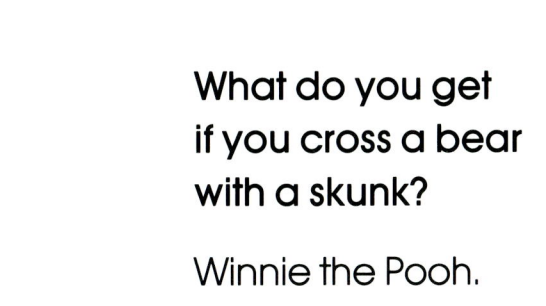

What do you get if you cross a bear with a skunk?

Winnie the Pooh.

What do you get if you cross an elephant with a kangaroo?

Great big holes all over Australia.

Why did the elephant paint his toe nails red?

Why is an elephant big, grey and wrinkly?

Because if he were small, white and round, he'd be an asprin.

So it could hide in the cherry tree.

How do you get four elephants in a car?

Two in the front and two in the back.

Why did the elephant paint himself different colours?
Because he wanted to hide in the crayon box.

Why did the cow go over the hill?

Because it can't go under it.

What do you call a bull asleep on the ground?

A bulldozer.

Where would you find a prehistoric cow?

In a moo-seum.

What goes OOM OOM?

A cow walking backwards.

TIC! TOC!

What goes tick-tock, bow-wow, tick-tock, bow-wow?

A watch dog.

What do you get if you pour hot water down a rabbit hole?

Hot-cross-bunnies.

Why are goldfish red?

The water makes them rusty.

What do baby apes sleep in?

Apricots.

Why didn't the viper vipe 'er nose?

What should you do if you find a snake in your bed?

Sleep on the wardrobe.

Because the adder 'ad 'er handkerchief.

What time is it when an elephant sits on the fence?

Time to fix the fence.

How do you know there's an elephant under your bed?

When your nose touches the ceiling.

What does an angry kangaroo do?

Gets hopping mad.

Why did the mother kangaroo scold her baby?

For eating biscuits in bed.

What did the big fire say to the little fire?

You're too young to smoke.

Son: "Can I have another glass of water?"

Father: "Another? This will be your tenth!"

Son: "I know, but my room's on fire."

What's white, has four legs and a trunk?

A mouse going on holiday.

What's brown, has four legs and a trunk?

A mouse coming back from holiday?

When is it bad luck to be followed by a black cat?

When you're a mouse.

What do angry mice send each other at Christmas?

Cross-mouse cards.

What kind of noise annoys an oyster?

What is black and white and very noisy?

A skunk with a drum kit.

A noisy noise annoys an oyster.

What's green and hairy and goes up and down?

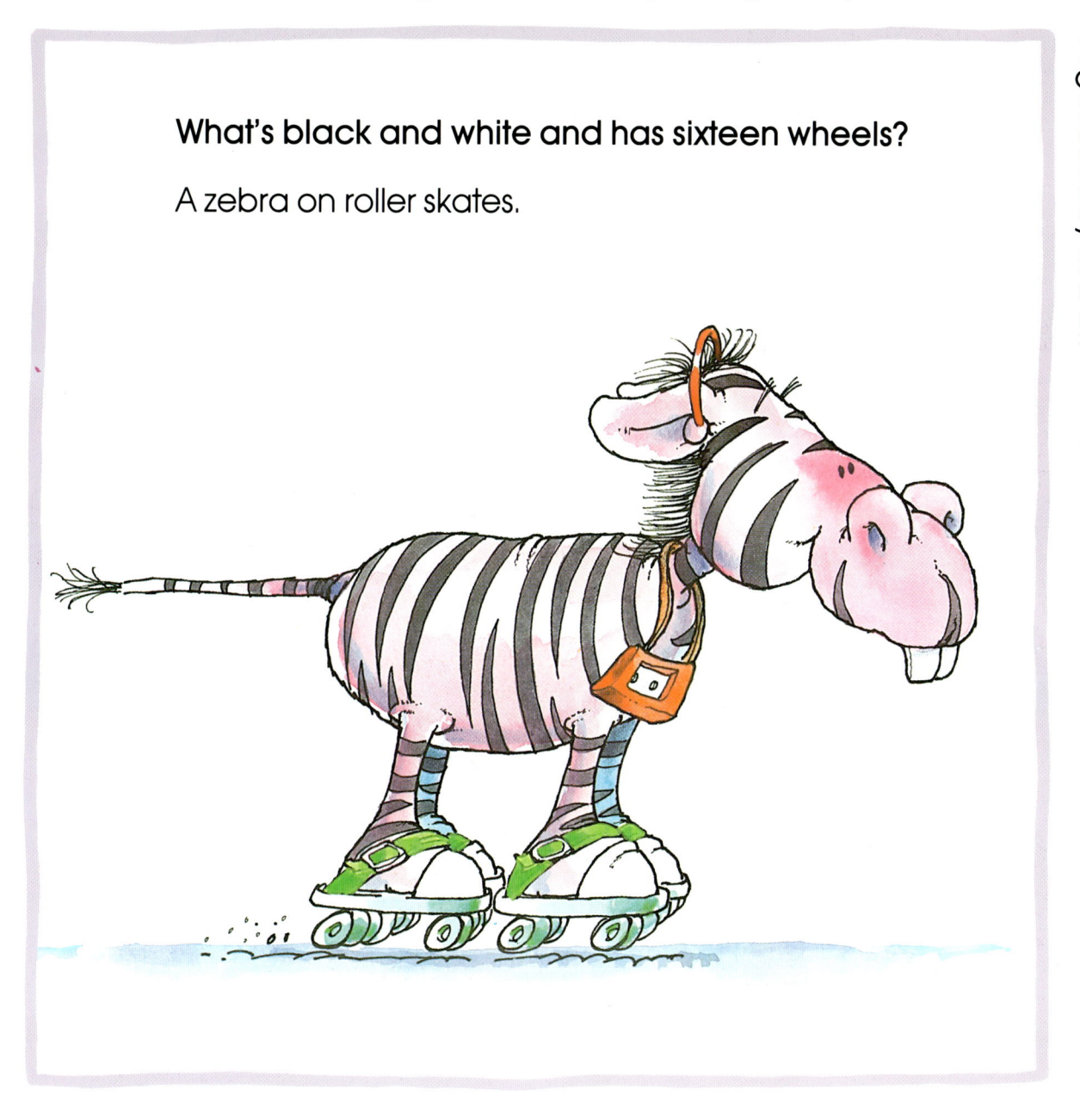

What's black and white and has sixteen wheels?

A zebra on roller skates.

A gooseberry in a lift.

There are ten copycats in a car, one gets out, how many are left?

None.

If I give you three rabbits —

— and then I give you two rabbits —

— how many rabbits do you have?

Six.

Six?

Yes, I've got one already.

What's green and has 400 wheels?

A centipede on roller skates.

If I had eight hedgehogs in one hand and seven hedgehogs in the other, what would I have?

Big hands.

Why do bees hum?

Because they don't know the words.

How do you start a flea race?

1, 2, flea, go.

What's green and dangerous and good at sums?

A crocodile with a calculator.

How do you stop a skunk smelling?

Hold its nose.

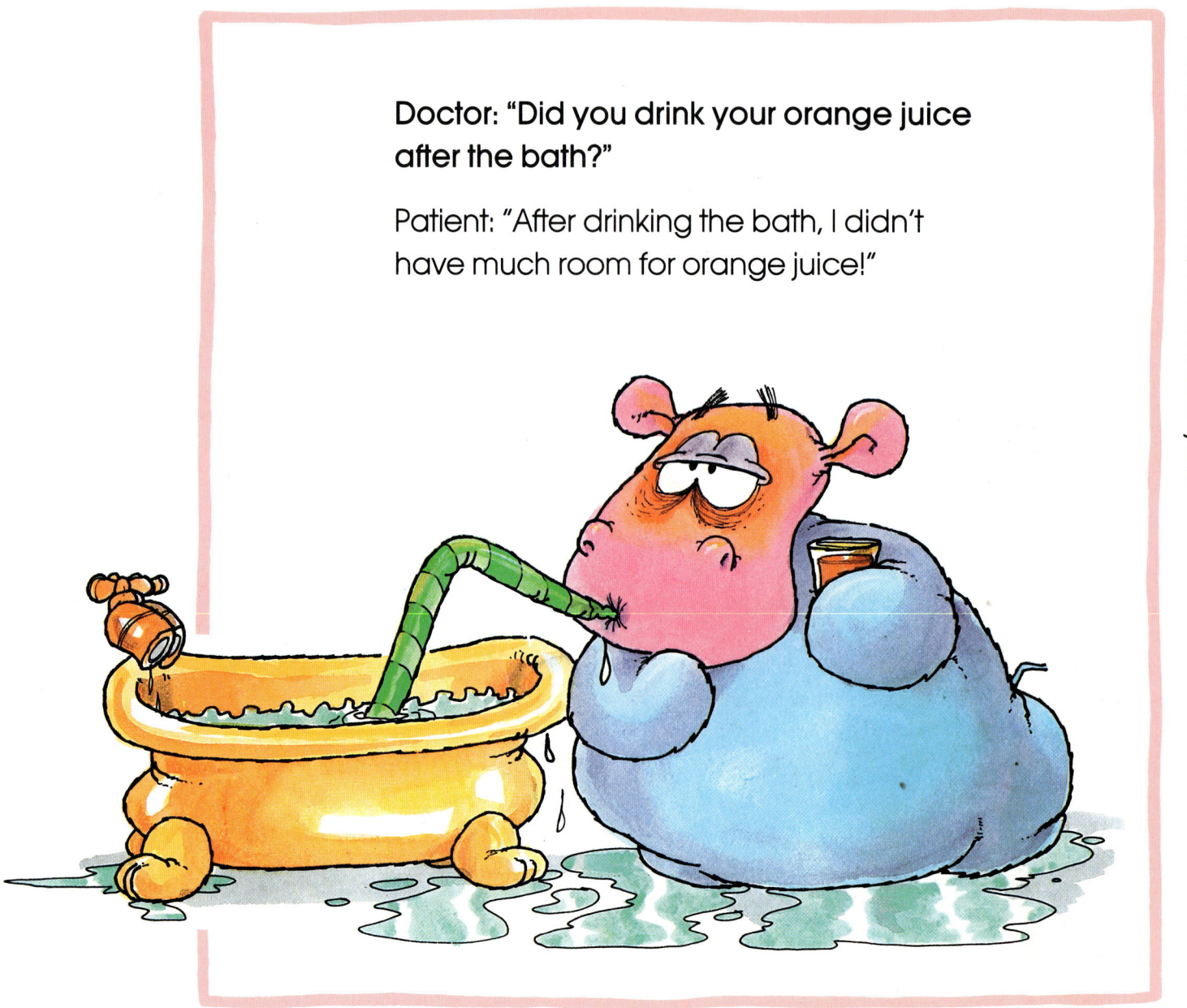

"Doctor, doctor, I feel like an apple."

Doctor: "Did you drink your orange juice after the bath?"

Patient: "After drinking the bath, I didn't have much room for orange juice!"

"Come over here, I won't bite you."

"Doctor, doctor, I keep thinking I'm a dustbin."

Patient: "Doctor, doctor, I keep forgetting things."

Doctor: "When did this start happening?"

Patient: "When did what start happening?"

"Don't talk rubbish."

A giraffe, an elephant, a camel, a bear, a monkey, a pig and a frog, two mice and a snake all sheltered under one umbrella – how many got wet?

None,
it wasn't raining.